CN00945052

NATIONAL THEATRE OF BR]

Conceived and created in 1979, the *National Theatre of Brent* has become something of a legend in the British theatre for its two-man epic re-enactments of myth and history. These include *The Charge of the Light Brigade, Zulu!, The Black Hole of Calcutta, Wagner's Ring, The Messiah, The Complete Guide to Sex, The Greatest Story Ever Told, The Mysteries of Sex* and *Love Upon the Throne*. Television appearances include an adaptation of *The Messiah* and the comedy series *Mighty Moments from World History* for Channel 4 and their award-winning *French Revolution* for BBC2. For BBC Radio 4, they have presented versions of the company's two other published works, *Shakespeare – the Truth! – the Complete History of the Bard* and *All the World's A Globe - the Entire History of the Universe* for which they won the Sony Radio Award and the Premier Ondas Award for European Comedy. Future plans include a World Tour, a new and expanded version of the *Brent Mystery Cycle* and a *History of the Twentieth Century*. N.B. Desmond and Raymond's *Shakespeare: the Masterclass* is available for lucrative private functions.

PATRICK BARLOW

Besides playing Desmond Olivier Dingle, Artistic Director of the National Theatre of Brent, recent theatre appearances include Humphry in Simon Gray's *Common Pursuit* (Phoenix), Sid in Ben Elton's *Silly Cow* (Haymarket) and Toad in Alan Bennett's version of *Wind in the Willows* (RNT). Television appearances include *Victoria Wood, French and Saunders, Absolutely Fabulous, Lovejoy, Class Act, Tales From the Crypt* and *Is It Legal*. Radio includes *The Diary of Adam and Eve, The Wizard of Oz* and regular appearances on *Quote Unquote* and *Looking Forward to the Past*. Recent films include *Shakespeare in Love* and *Notting Hill*. Other theatre and TV writing includes the *Life and Times of Purcell, True Adventures of Christopher Columbus, Queen of the East* and *Van Gogh*, for which he won a Silver Bear at the Berlin Film Festival, and the *The Judgement of Paris* for the ROH Garden Venture.

JOHN RAMM (Raymond Box)

Love Upon the Throne is John's third show with the National
Theatre of Brent. He created the part of Raymond for *The
Mysteries of Sex and Shakespeare – the Truth!* in 1997. Theatre
appearances include: three years at the Sheffield Crucible,
Hamlet, Have, Epicoene (Royal Shakespeare Co.); *The Tempest*
(Phoebus Cart); *Great Expectations* (Oxford Stage Co.); *The
Coal Dust Affair* (Actors Touring Co.); *Rent, What Must They
Think?* (Monstrous Regiment); *Beulah Land* (ICA); *The Nose,
The Cabinet of Doktor Caligari* (Nottingham Playhouse); *Time
and the Room* (Nottingham Playhouse and Edinburgh Inter-
national Festival); *Measure for Measure* (Nottingham Playhouse
and Barbican Theatre); *An Inspector Calls* (Garrick Theatre).
Opera includes: *Cherubin* (Royal Opera House) and *The
Threepenny Opera* (Scottish Opera). Television includes:
*The Wall Game; The Bill; Interrogation of John; South of the
Border*. Film includes: Stephen Poliakoff's *Food of Love* and
Tom Stoppard's *Shakespeare in Love*.

MARTIN DUNCAN

Opera productions include: *Ariadne auf Naxos* (Scottish
Opera/Edinburgh International Festival); *Albert Herring*
(Canadian Opera Co.); *Xerxes* (Bavarian State Opera, Munich);
The Magic Flute (Scottish Opera/Royal Opera House); *The
Thieving Magpie, Orpheus in the Underworld* (Opera North);
H.M.S. Pinafore, Die Fledermaus (D'Oyly Carte); *The Barber
of Seville* (English Touring Opera) and *The Judgement of Paris*
(ROH Garden Venture). As director of The National Theatre of
Brent: *The Greatest Story Ever Told* (Tricycle Theatre,
Edinburgh Festival and BBC Radio); *The French Revolution*
(BBC TV); *All the World's a Globe* (Sony Radio Award winner)
and *The Mysteries of Sex* (Nottingham Playhouse). In 1994,
Martin was appointed Artistic Director of Nottingham
Playhouse. His productions there include: Gogol's *The Nose,
The Cabinet of Doktor Caligari, Happy End* (co-production with
Edinburgh International Festival) and *The Adventures of
Pinocchio* (co-production with Teatro Kismet, Italy).

The National Theatre of Brent

presents

LOVE UPON
THE THRONE

by
PATRICK BARLOW

with additional material by

JOHN RAMM and MARTIN DUNCAN

London

A Nick Hern Book

Love Upon The Throne first published in Great Britain in 1998
as a paperback original by Nick Hern Books Limited,
14 Larden Road, London W3 7ST

Front cover: John Ramm and Patrick Barlow in *Love Upon The
Throne*. Photo: Matthew Ward

Typeset by Country Setting, Woodchurch, Kent TN26 3TB

Printed and bound in Great Britain
by Cox and Wyman, Reading RG1 8EX

ISBN 1 85459 421 4

A CIP catalogue record for this book is available from
the British Library

**A Personal Word from the
Artistic Director of the National Theatre of Brent**

Dear Theatrelover,

This is just a note to welcome you personally to the many and numerous treasures that lie embedded in this fascinating and evocative text.

I would also like to say that it took an immense amount of hard work penning this my latest magnum opus into the early hours, and also having to train up my trainee and assistant Raymond Box simultaneously at the same time.

In other words what I'm saying is, every word has been hand-picked, not to say manually wrenched, from the depths of my unconcious being, *so I'd be very grateful*, if you want to do a home-reading with your family and friends, that you don't start mucking about with it and changing things willy nilly.

There now follows a recent extract from my own fascinating personal and private diaries which – *at no extra cost* – is included in this volume.

Thank you.

Yours sincerely,

*Desmond Oliver Dingle
(author)*

Desmond Olivier Dingle,
Dollis Hill, 1998

For Sam and Joe

**An Exclusive Extract from the Secret Diaries of
Desmond Olivier Dingle**

A Week at the Edinburgh Festival

Monday   Hugely excited to be invited back to the Edinburgh
Fringe Festival and Tattoo to present my latest award-winning
Magnus Opus *Love upon the Throne* – the story of Charles
and Diana and their romance, marriage and divorce. Catch the
half ten all night video coach to Edinburgh. Hope Raymond
has remembered all our props many of which are very costly
replica Royal hats and artifacts, including a complete replica
Royal Throne of State from Westminster Abbey, incorporating
the controversial Stone of Scone which is extremely heavy
obviously and takes up most of the coach luggage facilities.
Raymond agrees to leave toboggan behind. Tedious ten hour
conversation explaining to Raymond that the Fringe Festival is
not a hairdressers' convention. Seven hour stop-over in
Peterborough.

Tuesday   At last find accommodation which is further from
the Centre than anticipated. All the same, Berwick-in-Tweed
is a lively and fascinating city with a wide variety of shops,
boutiques and restaurants to suit all tastes. For budgetry
reasons, Raymond and I are in a double room which has an
attractive view of Hadrian's Wall but is somewhat cramped.
Fail to understand why he *simply cannot accept and appreciate*
that an Artistic Director and Maison D'Etre of a National
Theatre Company should automatically get the top bunk.
Sir Peter Hall and Sir Trevor Nunn always get the top bunk
(not together obviously).

Wednesday   Busy day. 10.00 a.m: First Read Through and
Leafletting. 11.00 a.m: Elevenses. 12.00 a.m: Scott Monument
and Sightseeing. 13.00: Lunch – I have traditional Scottish fare

of Haggis and Neeps. Raymond has Haggis and Scampi. 14.00 p.m: Get-in and Full Technical Rehearsal. Raymond makes an embarrassing song and dance about having to carry all the props and the throne on his own. I take up valuable technical time patiently and generously explaining to him that as he is also the Stage Manager, carrying the set is one of his more obvious duties. 14.15 p.m: Full Dress Rehearsal. Now certain that my empathetic and sensitive portrayal of His Royal Highness Prince Charles will be a glorious triumph. It is sadly all too apparent, however, that Raymond has no acting skills whatsoever and cannot remember a single line. My worst fears confirmed. His portrayal of Diana will be a disaster. I only hope I can carry him (not literally obviously).

Thursday   Unfortunate mishap prevents us from appearing at our own First Night. Raymond thoughtlessly loses his toupee on the bus and we are forced to collect it from the Lost Property office at Galashiels Bus Terminal.

Friday   No reviews obviously. Arrive at the Edinburgh Royal Assembly Rooms where we are performing. Appalled to discover that we are expected to share our dressing room space with numerous other artists. Our dressing table is next to the Lady Boys of Bangkok. Raymond refuses to heed my warnings and strikes up an instant rapport. I myself have a fascinating theatrical conversation with Edward Petherbridge an illustrious actor from the RSC performing something called *Ted's Last Krapp* by Margaret Beckett. First show at 16.30 hours. Immense success. The Apotheosis of my Career. Searing notes session straight after the performance in which I help Raymond come to terms with his appalling and all too apparent inadequacies. First Night Party which I had hoped would be a quiet and reflective affair. A chance for me to recount encouraging stories and anecdotes of my numerous past successes and glories. However Raymond has invited not only thirty-two Lady Boys but the entire combined casts of *Disco Pigs, Poppy Tarts* and *I Licked a Slag's Deodorant.*

Saturday   Very unpleasant scenes over breakfast. Raymond announces he is going solo.

LOVE UPON THE THRONE

Love Upon the Throne was first staged in August 1998 in the
Assembly Rooms at the Edinburgh Festival and subsequently
at the Bush Theatre, London. The cast was as follows:

DESMOND OLIVIER DINGLE	Patrick Barlow
RAYMOND BOX	John Ramm

Directed by Martin Duncan
Designed by Francis O'Connor
Lighting by Chris Ellis

Plush red curtains hang around the stage in voluminous red folds. In the centre is a pair of golden doors. On either side there is an entrance through the curtains. On stage is an ornate table, two ornate chairs and – placed on eight unequal Doric columns – a royal handbag, a gold telephone, a flowery hat, a mobile phone, a dinner gong, a model train, a riding hat and a lifeguard's hat. In front of the whole set is a rope barrier with two notices that say: 'Please refrain from walking on the carpet.'

Play-in music ends.

Two USHERS *remove the barrier.*

Music: Prelude to 'The Ten Commandments'.

DESMOND *enters through the side curtains. Over his suit he is wearing the robes and feathered hat of the Prince of Wales for his investiture as the Prince of Wales.*

There is an enthusiastic round of applause.

He stands there waiting for the music to end. It goes on. DESMOND *signals to the* TECHNICIAN *behind the audience. The* TECHNICIAN *does not understand. The music goes on.* DESMOND *mouths into the darkness. He finally has to resort to an elaborate turn off the music gesture. The music snaps off embarrassingly.*

DESMOND. Good evening and welcome to this historic and attractive venue for tonight's performance of 'Love Upon the Throne'. Performed in its entirety by the Royal National Theatre of Brent, tackling for the first time in its history a more modern and contemporary theme from the annals of our own epoch. But first some introductions. I am Desmond Olivier Dingle, the author of tonight's work and also Artistic Director and Chief Executive of the Royal National Theatre of Brent. The Maison d'Etre if you will of the company's artistic policies. Now before we begin, I should like to just briefly mention our setting for the evening, designed by myself as it happens and based upon an actual replica of one of Her Majesty's many 'Drawing Rooms' that she has in Buckingham Palace for whenever she wishes to do some drawing. And in particular I would like to draw your attention to our fascinating display of royal hats and artifacts and in particular to our authentic replica royal throne of state that stands of course in Westminster Abbey and is made from virtually the same materials as the Royal Throne of State itself is made from, including a replica of the Stone of Scone. The famous Ston . . . from Scon. In fact many of these hats and artefacts will be actually used and handled during the show. So that's something to look forward to. Now I am sure that many of you will by now have noticed that I am in fact clothed in something rather unusual. For it is, in fact, my great honour to be modelling a replica of the actual garments worn by His Royal Highness His Royal Prince of Wales for his Investment as the Prince of Wales in Wales. This is, in fact, the only extant copy of the actual investment garments in existence. And to me these investment garments somehow represent if you will –

Enter RAYMOND *from stage left. He also wears the robes and feathered hat of the Prince of Wales.* DESMOND *does not see him.*

– not only the pomp and circumstance but also the simple dignity that our own Royal Family the House of Windsor has –

RAYMOND. Good evening ladies and gentlemen. Good evening Desmond. You will by now have noticed that I am clothed in something rather unusual.

DESMOND. Raymond?

RAYMOND. In fact, it is mine honour to be modellin' the only extinct replica of the actual garments worn by His Royal Highness –

DESMOND. Raymond!

RAYMOND. What?

DESMOND. I'm doin' the modellin'.

RAYMOND. I thought I was, Desmond.

DESMOND. No, I am now.

RAYMOND. Oh. Right.

DESMOND. So anyway . . . I suppose, before we continue,
I had better introduce the full acting company of the
Royal National Theatre of Brent – Raymond. Raymond . . .
um . . .

RAYMOND. Box.

DESMOND. Pardon?

RAYMOND. Box.

DESMOND. Box.

RAYMOND. Good evening ladies and gentlemen (*Bows.*)
Good evening Desmond.

DESMOND. Good evening.

RAYMOND. You will by now have noticed that I am clothed
in something –

DESMOND. Raymond! I am modelling the Investment
Garments!

RAYMOND. *But I was Desmond!!!*

DESMOND. Well you're not now, Raymond! Take them off!

RAYMOND. What?

DESMOND. Take them off!

RAYMOND *hurriedly takes off the investment garments.*

DESMOND. So now, without further ado, on with today's
performance. Would you prepare for the first scene please
Raymond?

RAYMOND. Certainly Desmond.

DESMOND. Thank you Raymond.

RAYMOND *carefully removes* DESMOND*'s investment garments. He forgets* DESMOND*'s gold tassle.*

DESMOND. Tassle.

RAYMOND. Pardon?

DESMOND. Tassle.

RAYMOND. No it's no trouble at all honestly.

DESMOND. No! Tassle!

RAYMOND. Right.

DESMOND. Re-enacting, as it does, possibly one of the most enthralling and romantic stories of all time. But first come back in time with us now to a time long gone by yet not so long gone as to be gone. Let us – in short – revisit one of the most fascinating epochs in recent years. I am of course referring to the 80s. Time of the . . . 80s.

RAYMOND. And where are we now pray but Buckingham Palace, set like a jewel in the midst of London's throbbing traffic in 1981.

DESMOND. Thank you.

DESMOND. And in this our first sequence –

RAYMOND. Desmond?

DESMOND. What?

RAYMOND. Is this when I do the dancing now Desmond?

DESMOND. What?

RAYMOND. The Javanese Temple Dance of the Dance of the seven –

DESMOND. No not now no! – the part of His Royal Highness the Prince of Wales will be enacted by . . . myself. Thank you. While Raymond will be taking the role of –

RAYMOND. – the young Javanese Temple Dancer in the dance of –

DESMOND (*taking handbag from plinth*). No!!! Her Majesty Queen Elizabeth II. In other words –

RAYMOND. The Q.E.II.

DESMOND (*sighs*). – the Monarch of the Glen . . . realm.

RAYMOND. Thank you.

> DESMOND *gives* RAYMOND *the handbag and exits through side curtains.* RAYMOND *sits on the throne. He is now the* QUEEN.

> DESMOND *knocks.*

RAYMOND. Come in.

> DESMOND *enters through the gold doors.*

DESMOND. Hello Your Majesty my Queen, the mother.

RAYMOND. Hello Prince Charles.

DESMOND. I believed you summonsed me to the Brown Windsors Throne room, Your Highness.

RAYMOND. That is indeed correct Prince Charles. I most certainly did. And I shall come straight to the point.

> *Awkward pause.*

As you know I am Her Royal Highness Queen Elizabeth II, the Majesty of the Queen of England.

DESMOND. You certainly are mine mother.

RAYMOND. Anyway, Your Father the Duke of Phillips and myself your mother and the Queen Mother my mother the mother of the Queen mother has been talking with the Parliament that it has recently come to our notice that you are rapidly approachin' middle age and are still not wed.

DESMOND. Yes um –

RAYMOND (*carries on*). Thus we was wonderin' when you might deign to receive the Sacrament of Holy Matrimony. And take the opportunity of continuing the mighty line of the House of Fraser. But there is a more important thing to say –

DESMOND. Windsor.

RAYMOND. Pardon?

DESMOND. Windsor.

RAYMOND (*realising*). Windsor!

DESMOND (*hastily*). Yes mother?

RAYMOND. Shit!

DESMOND. Yes mother?

RAYMOND. I know what it is! I knew what it was!

DESMOND. Yes mother?

RAYMOND. Shit!

DESMOND. Thank you Raymond. Yes mother? (*Prompting.*)
Are you not aware – *Will you try and remember your lines
please Raymond!!*

RAYMOND. *I only got them today, Desmond.*

DESMOND. *Are you not aware –*

RAYMOND (*remembering*). Are you not aware you are Prince
Charles King of Wales Charles, and therefore next in line to
the throne?

DESMOND. Am I?

RAYMOND. Do you not see the implements and relics of
Glorious Royalty arraigned upon these ancient walls?

DESMOND. I do yes. Where do they come from by the way?

RAYMOND. They have been here since time in a murial to
remind us of our inheritance. Look! (*They look up.*) Here is
the Albans Centre.

DESMOND. Orb and sceptre.

RAYMOND. Orbant semptre.

DESMOND (*sighs*). And lo! Therewithal the crown!

RAYMOND. The Crown of Jewels.

DESMOND. The Crown of England!

RAYMOND. The Crown of England! And the Crown of Jewels.

DESMOND. The Crown Jewels.

RAYMOND. The Crown Jewels of the Crown of England.

DESMOND. How beauteous they are.

RAYMOND. Yes! And look! There is the Star of India! And the Queen's Garter! And the Ruby Tuesday! And shall I now tell you what all this is, Charles?

DESMOND. Yes please.

RAYMOND. What all this is?

RAYMOND *does some mystic movements.*

DESMOND. What all this is!

RAYMOND. What all this is.

RAYMOND *clonks* DESMOND *with his handbag.*

DESMOND. Ow! Careful with your handbag Raymond!

RAYMOND. Sorry Desmond.

DESMOND. Carry on please Raymond.

Pause.

RAYMOND. It's your line.

DESMOND. No it's not.

RAYMOND. What?

DESMOND. Carry on please Raymond.

RAYMOND. It's your line.

DESMOND. What the hell are you on about!?

RAYMOND. What?

DESMOND. Will you get on with it!

RAYMOND. I am Desmond!!!

DESMOND. Then say the line!!!

RAYMOND (*exasperated*). It's your line!

DESMOND. IT'S NOT MY LINE!!!

RAYMOND. No! That's the line! It's Your Line is the line!!!!!

DESMOND. Good. Right. I was aware of that thank you
Raymond. So just give me the line again please.

RAYMOND. What line?

DESMOND. 'It's your line.'

RAYMOND. Is it?

DESMOND. Say the line!

RAYMOND. What line? I don't know what the hell we're
doin' now Desmond!

DESMOND. 'It's your line.'

RAYMOND. I just said it!

DESMOND. Well say it again!

RAYMOND. What?

DESMOND. 'IT'S YOUR LINE!'

RAYMOND. 'IT'S YOUR LINE!'

DESMOND. Thank you. Yes. I know it's my line my mother.

RAYMOND. So stop gallivanting about havin' a life of Old
Mother Riley with all the sexy starlets you've been seeing
such as George the fourth.

DESMOND. Susan George.

RAYMOND *none the wiser.*

RAYMOND. Susan George the fourth.

DESMOND. Susan George and so forth!

RAYMOND. Right. And become wed immediately to a
suitable young girl.

DESMOND. Very well I will. I will go about and think up
someone suitable in my opinion.

RAYMOND. We have already thought of someone in fact.

DESMOND. Who has?

RAYMOND. Me and the Dukes of Edinburgh. And we have invited her over for afternoon tea.

DESMOND. Very well, but before that I will ride upon mine horse in Hyde Park.

RAYMOND. Do not go far.

DESMOND. No just to the corner and back.

RAYMOND. Goodbye then.

DESMOND. Goodbye Your Highness.

Music: March from 'Incidental Music to Henry VIII'
by Sullivan.

DESMOND. And so it was that Prince Charles did ride upon his horse Red Rum round Hyde Park Corner and there it was that he did chance upon an lady also on upon her horse named Black Beauty. The Lady's name the Honourable Camilla Parker Knoll – she whose name would become legend in our legend here today here at this ancient and historic theatrical venue.

RAYMOND *takes the riding hat and comes on as* CAMILLA PARKER KNOLL. *He mimes trotting on a horse.*
DESMOND *mimes trotting on a horse too. They trot side by side.*

RAYMOND (*waving*). Hello Prince Charles!

DESMOND. Hello!

RAYMOND. Are you Prince Charles?

DESMOND. I am as it happens yes. And who might you be might I'n ask?

RAYMOND. Camilla Parker Knoll.

DESMOND. That's a very attractive name.

RAYMOND. Thank you.

DESMOND. In fact you're very attractive.

RAYMOND. Thank you. So anyway so are you if you want to know.

DESMOND. Me?

RAYMOND. Yes.

DESMOND. Good Heavens!

RAYMOND. With the perfectly honed physique of a Greek God. Every silky smooth tendon taut and tight to the touch.

DESMOND. Raymond!

RAYMOND. Oh, who could not wish to run their fingers over your lovely long tendrils –

   DESMOND *stops trotting.*

DESMOND. Raymond! We cut that actually!

   RAYMOND *stops trotting.*

RAYMOND. We never!

   They resume trotting.

DESMOND. So would you mind if I come straight to the point?

RAYMOND. No.

DESMOND. Then will you marry me Queen Parker Knoll?

RAYMOND. Unfortunately I'm afraid that I am already happen to be married.

DESMOND. But to whom might I'n ask?

RAYMOND. Whom to'm?

DESMOND. Yes.

RAYMOND. To my husband Colonel Sir Parker Knoll.

DESMOND. Damn!

RAYMOND. Bloody hell!

   Their horses suddenly become skittish and gallop out of control across the stage. They manage to subdue their steeds and trot back into position.

DESMOND. I cannot bear to think of you in another man's Weddin' Dress.

RAYMOND. Neither can I!

DESMOND. Because I now know that I love you!

RAYMOND. Yes! I love you too!

DESMOND (*suddenly awkward*). Thank you.

RAYMOND (*suddenly awkward*). Thank you.

DESMOND. Goodbye.

DESMOND. Goodbye.

> *They trot off to either side of the stage.* RAYMOND *removes his riding hat and collects the royal handbag.*

> *They are back in Buckingham Palace.* RAYMOND *sits on the throne.*

DESMOND. Hello Mother.

RAYMOND. Hello Prince Charles. Are you ready for your tea?

DESMOND. Yes please. However it is my honour to inform you that I have just met a young lady and I do wish to be wed with her.

RAYMOND. Young lady? What young lady?

DESMOND. Camilla Parker-Knoll is her name your Highness. Wife to Colonel Sir Parker-Knoll.

RAYMOND. The well-known manufacturer of the popular and attractive reclining sofa?

DESMOND. Yes.

RAYMOND. Don't be ridiculous, Charles!

DESMOND. What?

RAYMOND. That is completely out of the question! Look what happened last time!

DESMOND. Last time? What happened last time?

RAYMOND. All that Edward the Fox and Mrs Simpson business. It was a very very unpleasant situation. I'm sorry Charles! But you will have to give her up unfortunately. So as not to lose the trust of the Nation.

DESMOND. Give her up for the National Trust?

RAYMOND. Yes! Because anyway, as I was saying we have actually invited over a suitable young girl for the week-end for a spot of pheasant hunting in the grounds of Buckingham Palace.

DESMOND. Are we allowed to hunt pheasants in the grounds of Buckingham Palace?

RAYMOND. Of course. We are the Royal Family.

DESMOND. But –

RAYMOND (*announces*). But soft! I believe I can hear her knockin' on the door.

DESMOND *knocks on the royal table.*

RAYMOND. But anyway I'm goin' out now.

DESMOND. You're going out?

RAYMOND. Yes, I have to pop out for a moment to conduct the State Opening of The Parliament. So if you wouldn't mind just answering the door.

RAYMOND *exits hastily through the curtains.*

DESMOND. Come in?

The golden doors open. RAYMOND *appears as* DIANA.

RAYMOND. Your Royal Highness, may I present myself, I am the Most Honourable Princess Diana Lady Spencer.

DESMOND. Hello.

RAYMOND. Hello.

DESMOND. Won't you come in?

RAYMOND. Thank you.

RAYMOND *enters the room, looking about him.*

DESMOND. So is this your first trip to The Buckingham Palace?

RAYMOND. Indeed it is, my loyal leige.

DESMOND. Do you have any questions at all you'd like to ask at this juncture?

RAYMOND. Yes I do as it happens. By whom was it built?

DESMOND. By the Duke of Buckingham.

RAYMOND. Thank you. And he was from?

DESMOND. Buckingham.

RAYMOND. Thank you.

DESMOND. Ah! That sounds like tea-time. Thankyou Raymond.

   RAYMOND *beats gong.*

RAYMOND. Thankyou.

DESMOND. The rest of the Royal Family will now be gathering in the tea-rooms. So unfortunately I will now have to go now and take tea with the Royal Family. So anyway thank you for comin' and I hope everything works out and –

RAYMOND. Um actually I believe I was invited to take tea with the Royal Family myself.

DESMOND. Was you?

RAYMOND. Yes.

DESMOND. Right. So would you care to follow me please?

RAYMOND. Yes please.

DESMOND. So let us now proceed into the Royal Tea Rooms.

RAYMOND. Where they saw the famous Javanese Temple Dance of the Dance of the seven –

DESMOND. No Raymond!!

RAYMOND. What is it now then?

DESMOND. Tea isn't it?

RAYMOND. Tea? But we've only just started.

DESMOND. The Tea *Scene!*

RAYMOND. The Tea *Scene!*

Music: 'The Haunted Ballroom' by Toye.

The table is now the royal tearooms. They sit down at it.
RAYMOND *slides the handbag down the table.*
DESMOND *grabs the handbag and becomes the* QUEEN.

DESMOND. So, Lady Di –

RAYMOND. Yes?

DESMOND. Are you enjoying taking afternoon tea with the Royal Family?

RAYMOND. Yes thank you.

DESMOND. Would you care for anything further to eat?

RAYMOND. Piece of cake please.

DESMOND. Certainly. Anyway as you know I am now Her Majesty the Queen.

RAYMOND. Yes.

DESMOND. And I should now like to introduce you to the rest of the Royal Family. Her Royal Highness my mother the Queen Mother, His Royal Highness his husband my Philip Duke of Edinburgh, Prince Andrew Duke of Yorks, Princess Margaret Duke of Earl, Princess Anne Theatre Royal, Princess Michael of Michael and of course His Royal Highness Prince Charles and Heir to the throne of England, the United Kingdom, the British Commonwealth and all her proud dominions.

RAYMOND. Lovely.

DESMOND. So anyway, Lady Di. What do you do then?

RAYMOND. Well, your Royal Highness the Queen, I am currently working in a small posh nursery doing nursery nursing which I very much enjoy.

DESMOND. Nursery nursing?

RAYMOND. Yep.

DESMOND. So do you have any other ambitions of any form?

RAYMOND. No.

A slightly awkward moment.

DESMOND. So that leaves the nursery nursing which is enjoyable but you're not necessarily (*Pointed.*) . . . wedded to it.

LADY DI *begins to get the* QUEEN*'s drift.*

RAYMOND. No . . . I wouldn't say . . . wedded to it, no.

DESMOND. So anyway Prince Charles – talking of weddin's – Oh! Where is Prince Charles? He seems to have inadvertently left the table surreptitiously.

RAYMOND. Oh!

DESMOND. Hang on a sec. What d'you say Prince Andrew? He's on the what? He's on the terrace? On the telephone? Princess Anne, would you go and tell Prince Charles to – I beg your pardon? You haven't what? I don't care if you haven't finished your cake. Who's Queen here? I'm so sorry about this, Lady Di.

RAYMOND. That's perfectly all right, your Most Serene Highness, but would you allow me to go?

DESMOND. Oh. Very well. Sit down, Princess Anne. Lady Di will go.

RAYMOND. Thank you.

Opening of the 'Warsaw Concerto' – Addinsell.

DESMOND *places the handbag on its plinth. Then takes the mobile phone from the opposite plinth. There is a dramatic lighting change as he becomes* PRINCE CHARLES *shouting into the phone.*

DESMOND. Hello! Hello! This is Prince Charles here and I am trying to make an urgent call to the new wife of Brigadier Sir Major Sir Parker Knolls!

RAYMOND *appears as* LADY DI.

Yes!? What is it footman? (*Sees* LADY DI.) Oh!!

RAYMOND. Excuse me Your Royal Highness but I am not actually the footman. But the Honourable Princess Diana Lady Spencer.

DESMOND. I'm so sorry. I was just upon my new mobile telephone.

RAYMOND. A mobile telephone! I've never seen a mobile telephone before!

DESMOND. Yes we get a lot of gadgets before the general populace.

RAYMOND. Would you care for me to go away?

DESMOND. Um . . . look . . . I think I should probably explain –

RAYMOND. You look so sad and lost and lonely.

DESMOND. Pardon?

RAYMOND. My heart bled for you when I saw you this afternoon in the Big Throne Room of the Brown Windsors. I thought to myself: 'You are so lonely. It is wrong you are so lonely. That you should have someone to look after you and to care for you'. (CHARLES *looks at her.*) That is what I thought anyway . . .

DESMOND. Did you?

RAYMOND. I believe you have had a childhood starved of love as I have. I believe you have a deep emptiness that cannot be filled. And you are so sad and lost and lonely that you do not know where to turn and I am totally besotted by you.

They look at one another.

DESMOND. Would you care for another sausage?

RAYMOND. Pardon?

DESMOND. I'm so sorry, I thought for a moment we was at a barbecue.

An awkward moment.

So do you have any . . . hobbies at all?

RAYMOND. Nursery nursing.

DESMOND. Besides the nursery nursing.

RAYMOND. Right. Erm . . . I like pets. When I was young I had two guinea pigs.

DESMOND. I *too* had two guinea pigs!

RAYMOND. You too had two guinea pigs too?

DESMOND. Yes. And an elephant.

RAYMOND. An *elephant!!?*

DESMOND. On wheels obviously.

RAYMOND *laughs.*

DESMOND. Also a model train set and a Beatle wig.

RAYMOND. A wig made of *beetles?*

DESMOND. No. A 'Beatle' wig.

RAYMOND *looks blank.*

In other words a wig as worn by one of the 'Beatles' or Fab Four. The highly acclaimed popular pop duo.

RAYMOND. I have hundreds of fluffy toys and gonks and teddies and other humorous nick-nacks.

DESMOND (*unsettled*). Right.

RAYMOND. So do you like listening to music Charles?

DESMOND. I do actually yes. I like classical music very much.

RAYMOND. I like classical music too obviously but I particularly like all the popular pop groups of the time.

DESMOND. Yes of course I like modern popular pop music. In particular Diana Ross and the Three Degrees. Stop in the name of love.

RAYMOND. Pardon?

DESMOND (*helpfully*). Stop in the Name of Love.

RAYMOND. I think I have Charles. I think I have.

They are now gazing at one another.

DESMOND. Right. So I think I'd better . . . (*A moment of decision.*) . . . turn off my –

RAYMOND. – mobile telephone. Yes.

DESMOND. Right.

RAYMOND. Good.

DESMOND. Yes.

CHARLES turns off his mobile telephone. Immediately we hear again the opening bars of the 'Warsaw Concerto' – Addinsell.

DESMOND and RAYMOND march purposefully to stage left and right. DESMOND replaces the mobile phone on its plinth.

They march purposefully back again and turn to the audience.

DESMOND. And so it was to become more and more ever obvious to Royal pundits the world over that the Royal Couple was heading closer and closer to the state of Holy Matrimony. And almost immediately Charles and Di fever gripped the whole world.

RAYMOND. In particular Indonesia where Princess Diana and the Prince of Charles watched the famous –

DESMOND. No Raymond –

RAYMOND. – Javanese Temple Dance of the Dance of the Seven –

DESMOND. – Not yet!

RAYMOND. Not yet?

DESMOND. We're not in Java!

RAYMOND. Oh go on Desmond! I've been practising for –

DESMOND. No!

RAYMOND. Later though?

DESMOND (*unwillingly*). Yes.

RAYMOND. Later in the –

DESMOND. Yes!

RAYMOND. So what is it now then?

DESMOND. The News now isn't it?

RAYMOND. BBC?

DESMOND. Yeah.

BBC News music.

DESMOND *sits behind the table. Mimes arranging his papers till the music stops.*

DESMOND. Hello and here is the BBC News from the BBC. It is June the third nineteen . . . nineteen . . . in . . . the Nineteen Eighties. And I am your newsreader for this evening, Sir Alexandra Brunette. Hello. And I've just this minute been handed a very important piece of last minute news and – Yes! His Royal Highness the Prince Charles has just this minute proposed to her Ladyship Lady Di and she has said Yes Please! So now over straight away to Sir Peter Sissons who is at Buckingham Palace to talk to Lady Di.

DESMOND *is now* SIR PETER SISSONS. RAYMOND *joins him on the other side of the table as* LADY DI.

RAYMOND. Hello Lady Di.

DESMOND. No. You're Lady Di.

RAYMOND. Right.

DESMOND. Hello Lady Di.

RAYMOND. Hello.

DESMOND. I am Sir Peter Sissons.

RAYMOND. Hello.

DESMOND. Hello. Well this is very good news Your Royal Highness.

RAYMOND. Thank you.

DESMOND. Surprised at all?

RAYMOND. No.

DESMOND. So when's the happy day to be?

RAYMOND. The Nineteen . . . Eighties.

DESMOND (*ruthless*). And you're quite certain that pressure from the Royal Family and massive International and National Public Opinion didn't force him to make this decision against his will!?

RAYMOND. No.

DESMOND. Good. Well that's absolutely marvellous. So congratulations on behalf of the whole nation and all of us here at the BBC.

RAYMOND. Thank you.

DESMOND. And now back to the Studio. Goodbye.

RAYMOND. Goodbye.

BBC News music.

RAYMOND. And so it was that the Nation prepared for the Royal Wedding of Charles and Diana Spencer

DESMOND. No. Not Charles and Diana Spencer.

RAYMOND. It was!

DESMOND. No it was Charles. And Diana Spencer.

RAYMOND. That's what I said.

DESMOND. No you said Charles and Diana Spencer.

RAYMOND. Yes.

DESMOND. It's not Charles Spencer!

RAYMOND. Who isn't?

DESMOND. They wasn't married.

RAYMOND. They was!

DESMOND. No!! It was the the Royal Wedding of Charles! (*Exaggerated gesture.*) And Diana Spencer.

RAYMOND (*repeats*). The Royal Wedding of Charles! (*Exaggerated gesture.*) And Diana Spencer.

DESMOND. Yes.

RAYMOND. And so it was that the Nation prepared for the Royal Wedding of Charles! (*Exaggerated gesture.*) And Diana Spencer.

DESMOND. With such things as –

RAYMOND. Erm –

DESMOND. Street bunting –

RAYMOND. Street bunting.

DESMOND. And Fl –

RAYMOND. – the Javanese Temple Dance of the Dance of the Seven –

DESMOND. No!

RAYMOND. Owww! You said later!

DESMOND. Yes later! Not now!

RAYMOND. Why?

DESMOND. Look Raymond this is a finely crafted and delicately balanced piece of theatrical writing. You can't just bung in a temple dance whenever you feel like it!

RAYMOND. You're always bunging in stuff whenever you feel like it! You're bunging it in left right and centre!

DESMOND. Yes. I happen to be the chief dramaturge Raymond!

RAYMOND. Pardon?

DESMOND. Dramaturge. I can bung in what I want when I want!

RAYMOND. Right. So you just tell me when we're doin' it and I'll do it.

DESMOND. Right.

RAYMOND. Right!

DESMOND. Thank you.

RAYMOND. Thank you!

DESMOND. Thank you.

RAYMOND. No. Thank you!

> RAYMOND *scratches his head. His toupee slips.*
> DESMOND *looks appalled.* RAYMOND *is mortified.*

DESMOND. What the –

RAYMOND. It's alright Desmond thank you!

> RAYMOND *shoves his toupee back.*

DESMOND. Alright, Raymond –

RAYMOND. No, please thank you. Shit! Shit! Shit!

DESMOND. So anyway . . . um . . .

RAYMOND. No thank you! I'm alright now thank you!!

DESMOND. Um . . .

RAYMOND. I'd rather not discuss my cosmetic arrangements now thank you very much thank you.

DESMOND. Right –

RAYMOND. Thank you!!!! Carry on please!!!

DESMOND. Right Raymond.

RAYMOND. Right.

DESMOND. Whenever you're ready please.

RAYMOND. What?

DESMOND. Kindly let us proceed to the next sequence please Raymond.

RAYMOND. What sequence might that be please Desmond please?

DESMOND. The Prior to the Weddin' Arrangements Sequence Raymond.

RAYMOND. Thank you. And so it was, the whole Nation prepared for the Royal Wedding of Charles (*Exaggerated gesture.*) and Diana Spencer with such things as street bunting and the famous . . . (*Reminds himself.*) later! . . . and flags of all nations, while the Royal Couple made their own preparations, unbeknownst to the Common Folk of England, but just as important.

DESMOND *exits.*

RAYMOND *takes the royal gold telephone from its plinth and puts it on the table. He dials a number.*

Sound of telephone ringing.

DESMOND *appears. He is holding a handset.*

DESMOND. Hello.

RAYMOND. Hello. This is Princess Diana here. Are you David and Emmanuel Emmanuel?

DESMOND. We are yes.

RAYMOND. Would you like to make my Wedding Dress?

DESMOND. Yes please. Would you like it in white?

RAYMOND. No, in ivory to suit my skin tones.

DESMOND. Right.

RAYMOND. I would like it made of silk. With a twenty-five yard train.

DESMOND. Twenty-five yards?

RAYMOND. Yes please.

DESMOND. Um . . . twenty-five yards is in fact seventy-five feet which is, in fact, the size of two small football pitches laid end to –

RAYMOND. Twenty-five *foot* train!!

DESMOND. Thank you.

RAYMOND. And I should like three copies made please.

DESMOND. For posterity?

RAYMOND. No in case I get cake on it.

DESMOND. Fair enough.

RAYMOND. Thank you. Goodbye.

DESMOND. Goodbye.

> DESMOND *rushes out and reappears through the opposite curtains with the same handset.*

DESMOND. Hello.

RAYMOND. Hello. This is Princess Diana here.

DESMOND. This is Dame Kiri de Kanawa here.

RAYMOND. Hello is that Dame Kiri de Kanada?

DESMOND. Kanawa!

RAYMOND. Yes?

DESMOND. Yes, this is Dame Kiri here, yes.

RAYMOND. It's Princess Diana Spencer here, Dame Kiri.

DESMOND. Who?

RAYMOND. Princess Diana Spencer. Soon to be wed to Prince Charles. I hope I have not woken you.

DESMOND. Well it is half past three in the morning here in New Zealand.

RAYMOND. Sorry. Anyway I was wonderin' whether you would be prepared to sing at the Royal Wedding.

DESMOND. Yes, I certainly would.

RAYMOND. Thank you and good luck with your continuing career.

DESMOND. Thank you. (*Turns to* AUDIENCE.) Meanwhile at Highgrove Hall.

DESMOND exits. He reappears immediately without the handset. He now sits before the gold phone. His hand trembles over it before dialling a number.

Suddenly RAYMOND *appears behind him.* DESMOND *drops the handset guiltily.*

RAYMOND. Hello Charles!

DESMOND. Oh! Hello Diana! Whatchoo you doin' round here at my Royal Residence of Highgrove House?

RAYMOND. I just come round from the Queen Mother's where I am currently residing before the Royal Weddin' to show you my attractive new engagement costume. (DESMOND *looks blank.*) It is a lovely peacock blue.

DESMOND. Yes it certainly is. So you'rc going to wear that while we're engaged?

RAYMOND. Well not all the time obviously.

DESMOND. Well obviously, not all the time no!

RAYMOND. Are you alright Charles? You seem somewhat distracted somewhat.

DESMOND. No, I'm just very worried about . . . about the State of British architecture as it happens which is in a terrible state, in my opinion.

RAYMOND. You're not having second thoughts about . . . us?

DESMOND. Don't be ridiculous!

RAYMOND. You're not dreadin' it then?

DESMOND. What?

RAYMOND. Dreadin' the Weddin'?

DESMOND. Course I'm not dreadin' the Weddin'!

RAYMOND. See ya there then!

DESMOND. Okay!!

DESMOND. And now, Ladies and Gentlemen. We need to prepare for that happy and glorious moment when her great big Majesty Queen Elizabeth led the Royal couple and the entire Royal Family before all the populace of England and the entire world. And in order to re-evoke this historic moment, we shall now be asking you yourselves to play that grateful and euphoric populace.

House lights go up.

And for this sequence, we are going to divide the entire audience into three separate halves, groups or groupings. First the left half – which is Group No. A – is the left half of the auditorium.

RAYMOND *indicates in air steward style.*

So group No. A – you will now stand up and convey the traditional joyful salute of the common folk of England. Thank you Raymond.

RAYMOND. Hooray! Hooray! We the Common People say Hooray!!

AUDIENCE. Hooray! Hooray! We the Common People say Hooray!!

DESMOND. Very good indeed. Now we turn our attention to the second group or groupin' of the Audience. Group No. B. Which this time is the middle half of the auditorium. (RAYMOND *indicates.*) And you will utter exactly the same joyful salute, but in the proud language of Prince Charles himself – the language of Wales. Thank you Raymond.

RAYMOND *makes whale sounds.*

No Raymond!

RAYMOND. What?

DESMOND. In Welsh.

RAYMOND. Welsh!!

DESMOND. Yes!

RAYMOND. Sorry Desmond! Sorry!

DESMOND. Carry on please.

RAYMOND. Hooroo! Hooroo! Plaid Cymru! Hooroo!!

AUDIENCE. Hooroo! Hooroo! Plaid Cymru Hooroo!!

DESMOND. Now finally Group number C. The left block
of the audience. Or Eastern Bloc as we say in the theatre.
You will utter your joyful salute but in one of the most
popular tongues of the British Commonwealth. Australian.
Thankyou Raymond.

RAYMOND. 'Nice one Cobber. Fair Dinkum and Good on yer
Poms.'

DESMOND. Not too rowdy please. And don't forget to copy
Raymond with your antipodean gestures.

AUDIENCE. 'Nice one Cobber. Fair Dinkum and Good on yer
Poms.'

DESMOND. And now Raymond will pass amongst you with
our attractive hand-written and historically authenticated
quotations actually shouted out to the Happy Couple as they
passed by in the State Coach by certain leading world
leaders and celebrities of the time.

RAYMOND *gives out six cards to various audience
members.*

Raymond is now choosing certain members of the audience
according to various facial characteristics. Don't forget you
have been specifically selected by Raymond so kindly do
not attempt to pass your card to another member of the
audience or attempt to destroy it. Good. So are all our cards
delivered Raymond?

RAYMOND. Yes thank you Desmond.

DESMOND. So let's hear No 1. Stand up and shout out your historically authenticated quotation please. Thank you.

AUDIENCE NO. 1. 'Don't do anything I wouldn't do.'

DESMOND. That was the Pope. Thank you. Now number two please.

AUDIENCE NO. 2. Beaucoup de Felicitations!!

DESMOND. That was Gerard Depardieu. Thank you. And now number three.

AUDIENCE NO. 3. Love the shoes Your Highness!!

DESMOND. That was Imelda Marcos. Thank you. Now number four please.

AUDIENCE NO. 4. Fan-dabee-dozee!

DESMOND. That was Margaret Thatcher. Thank you. Now number five please.

AUDIENCE NO. 5. May I take this opportunity of sending many congratuluations on your recent nuptials on behalf of my husband and myself and we hope you will come and see us next time you're down our way.

DESMOND. That was the People of Belgium. Now finally number six please.

AUDIENCE NO. 6. Congratulations!

DESMOND. That was Sir Cliff Richard. Thank you. Actually I wonder if you would sing it please. Thank you. And now all of the quotations in succession please. And Go!

Selected AUDIENCE MEMBERS *shout out all six quotations in order.*

Right Groups A, B and C – remember your group phrases and numbers one to ten remember to shout out your greetings as and when you see your number. Thank you.

Music: 'Zadok the Priest'.

DESMOND. And so it was they done the Royal Wedding. And after the Royal Wedding the Royal couple rode in glorious procession along Horseguards Parade, through the Admiral's Archway and down the Strand, doing the Lambeth Walk obviously, till they reached Buckingham Palace and they stood upon the balcony and was greeted by greetings from all the people of the whole world.

RAYMOND. No. A. Please! No. B! No. C! Etc. Etc.

DESMOND. One! Two! Three! Etc. Etc.

The AUDIENCE *now enact the participatory celebration. After which* DESMOND *gives them a round of applause.*

RAYMOND *shifts the table.*

House lights go down again.

Music: Theme from 'The Onedin Line'.

DESMOND. And so it was that the newly-weds went on honeymoon on the Royal Yacht the Cutty Sark before returning to their first marital home of Highgrove House. (*He becomes* CHARLES.) Anyway Diana, here we are at Highgrove Home, your new house.

RAYMOND (*looking about him*). Very nice.

DESMOND. Highgrove House, your new home.

RAYMOND. Very nice too.

DESMOND. Thank you.

RAYMOND (*excited*). So what shall we do now then?

DESMOND. Well I'll be working in my office in here. See you later.

DESMOND *sits down at the table.* RAYMOND *mimes knocking.* DESMOND *knocks on the table but out of synch.*

DESMOND. Come in.

RAYMOND. What will you be doing exactly?

DESMOND. Affairs of State.

RAYMOND. Do you do affairs of State?

DESMOND (*defensive*). Yes.

RAYMOND. I thought the Government do Affairs of State.

DESMOND. I do and the Government do.

RAYMOND (*takes this in*). So what do I do then?

DESMOND. Whatever you want to do.

RAYMOND. What though?!

DESMOND. Keep your hair on Diana!

A moment of embarrassment.

DESMOND. Anyway, I must send a facsimile or 'fax' – as we call it – from my new facsimile machine to my mysterious godfather, mystic and mentor Sir Laurens Van der . . . Van der . . . Dick Van Dyke.

RAYMOND (*disappointed*). Right. Goodbye then.

DESMOND. Goodbye. And close the door please.

RAYMOND. Sorry.

RAYMOND mimes closing CHARLES's office door. He wanders into the gothic halls of Highgrove.

DESMOND *exits.*

RAYMOND. What will I do now? I know! I'll find the Royal Bedroom. And make myself at home.

RAYMOND exits through the gold doors. we hear him from offstage.

RAYMOND. Look at all these corridors and millions and millions of rooms to choose from. Where can it be I wonder?

RAYMOND enters again.

Ah! Here it is. (*Gasps.*) Look at this bedroom! Compared to the one I had in my bedsit. My own towelling bathrobe. Tea and coffee making facilities. A Corby trouser press!

Enter DESMOND. He wears a chambermaid's hat and apron.

DESMOND. Might I help you Madam?

RAYMOND. And who might you be, might I'n ask?

DESMOND. I am your own personal chambermaid.

RAYMOND. Chambermaid? Fancy having my own personal chambermaid to have at my own beck and callin'. Might I order you to do anything I fancy?

DESMOND. Well within reason obviously.

RAYMOND. Chambermaid?

DESMOND. Yes?

RAYMOND. You don't like being chambermaid do you Desmond?

DESMOND. Get on with it Raymond.

RAYMOND. Boot's on the other foot now isn't it?

DESMOND. Get on with it!

RAYMOND. Anyway, I should like to hear my favourite the latest popular hit record single by the Dire Straits pops groups.

DESMOND. Unfortunately, Your Highness, I'm afraid we are not at liberty to play popular music records at Highgrove Hall.

RAYMOND. On whose orders?

DESMOND. On the orders of Prince Charles. The Heir to the throne of Britain.

RAYMOND. Bloody hell! I never thought it would be like this being Princess Di!

DESMOND. I'm sorry but that's just the way it is!

Music: 'The City' from Psycho – Herrmann.

RAYMOND. Kindly fetch me a packet of half-coated digestive biscuits please if you would.

DESMOND. I'm not absolutely certain we have any packets of half coated –

RAYMOND. You get them! Do you hear!

DESMOND. Certainly Your Highness.

RAYMOND. Get those biscuits! Do you hear my command?!

An awkward moment as RAYMOND *starts melding with his character.*

DESMOND. Raymond!!

RAYMOND. Sorry Charles. Desmond. Chambermaid.

DESMOND *exits.* RAYMOND *moves the table.*

Music: fades.

DESMOND *enters. They now sit at either end of the table.*

RAYMOND. Well this is a novelty.

DESMOND. I beg your pardon?

RAYMOND. Having dinner together.

DESMOND. Yes. Anyway . . . um . . . I was hoping we might have a conversation concerning various philosophical issues, such as why we are here, for example.

RAYMOND. Pardon?

DESMOND. What is the purpose of our having been placed upon the world, in other words?

RAYMOND *looks blank.*

DESMOND. What is the meaning of life?

RAYMOND. I don't know!

DESMOND. Right. And another question.

RAYMOND. Yes?

DESMOND. What are all those fluffy toys and gonks and teddies and whatnot doing in our bedroom?

RAYMOND. They are all my fluffy toys, gonks and teddies and other humorous knicknacks. Do you not like them?

DESMOND. They're not to my personal taste to be honest, no.

RAYMOND. Might I have my pudding now please?

DESMOND. You've just had pudding.

RAYMOND. Another pudding please.

DESMOND. Should you be having so many puddings?

RAYMOND. Yes, if I want!!

DESMOND. Are you feeling alright Diana?

RAYMOND. I want to get away!

DESMOND. We've only just got here.

RAYMOND. I want to go on holiday.

DESMOND. Go on holiday! But I am the Prince of Wales. I have obligations to my Nation!

RAYMOND. I can't move! I can't breathe! Everything's closing in!

DESMOND. Alright! Alright!

RAYMOND. I want to get out!

DESMOND. Alright we will go on holiday!

RAYMOND (*calms down instantly*). Right. Thank you. How about the Bahamas?

DESMOND. Erm . . .

RAYMOND. Then on to Java, home of the famous Javanese Temple Dance of the –

DESMOND. RAYMOND! I was thinking more of Balmoral.

RAYMOND. Balmoral?

DESMOND (*excited*). To spend six whole weeks with the Royal Family and my mother the Queen.

RAYMOND (*appalled*). Six whole weeks with the whole Royal Family!!

Music: Prelude from 'Psycho',

They carry their seats to the front of the table. They are now travelling in the royal car. Doing bouncing car acting. CHARLES *is driving.* DIANA *staring anxiously ahead.*

RAYMOND. Oh no! Balmoral! What am I going to do? Is there no escape? I thought I'd married a man. But I have married a whole Dynasty!

DESMOND (*changing gear*). It will be lovely in Balmoral won't it, Diana?

RAYMOND. Yes, it will yes.

DESMOND. All the heather and the grouse shooting and the Scottish country dancing we do every night after dinner. Not to mention Princess Margaret's hilarious impressions! Which'll have us all in stitches I can tell you.

RAYMOND. Lovely! (*Aside.*) Oh no! Country dancing! I hate country dancing! What am I going to do!!! I feel I'm close to panic! I love you Charles! I love you!

DESMOND. Thank you very much.

RAYMOND. Do you love me?

DESMOND. Of course I love you, Diana. Whatever 'love' may mean.

RAYMOND. Thank you.

DESMOND. Are you alright Diana? You're looking a little highly strung.

RAYMOND. No I'm fine thank you. I am perfectly alright.

DESMOND. Good.

Psycho music ends.

They sit round the table again. RAYMOND *throws the handbag at* DESMOND. DESMOND *catches it and becomes the* QUEEN *again..*

DESMOND. So, anyway –

RAYMOND *is still doing the bouncing car acting.*

We're not in the car now Raymond.

RAYMOND. Sorry Desmond.

DESMOND. So anyway how are you enjoying your holiday staying with the Royal Family at Balmoral Lady Di?

RAYMOND. Very much thank you Your Majesty.

DESMOND. And you know everybody of course? (*Goes round table.*) Queen Mother, Prince Edward, Princess Anne, Princess Andrew, Queen Mother, Princess Margaret. She's a card, isn't she? Those impressions! Dear oh dear! (*Laughs like a drain.*) Prince Charles – obviously, huh! You should know him by now. Hope you do anyway! And our latest addition – the Duchess of York. Or as we call her of course – Yorkie.

RAYMOND *nods to* FERGIE.

So, anyway, I gather you might have some glad tidings Diana.

RAYMOND. I do, yes, Your Highness as it happens. It is my honour to announce I am having a little baby.

DESMOND. Having a little baby? Congratulations, Lady Di.

RAYMOND. Thank you. But I want to make one thing quite clear.

DESMOND. Yes? What is it? You're suddenly looking very headstrong.

RAYMOND. As soon as I have had the baby at St Mary's Paddington Station, I have decided I am going on a world tour of Austria and New Zealand with my husband! In case I'm feeling a bit depressed.

DESMOND. With the little baby!!

RAYMOND. Yes! And no-one's going to stop me!

Music: Lutoslawski – Chain – A Battuta.

Music fades.

DESMOND *is* **PRINCE CHARLES** *and* **RAYMOND** *the* **PRIME MINISTER** *of Australia and New Zealand.*

RAYMOND. Welcome, Your Highness. I am Prime Minister of
Austria and New Zealand. May I welcome you to my
countries.

DESMOND. Thank you, Prime Minister. Well, may I just say –

RAYMOND. But where is your new wife My Highness?

DESMOND. She's just on her way. Powdering her nose
probably. You know what these women are like! Ha! ha! ha!

Music: Bach's Orchestral Suite No. 3 in D. Air.

RAYMOND *suddenly gazes before him and gasps.*

RAYMOND. And is this your wife Your Highness?

DESMOND. Yes it is.

RAYMOND. Good Heavens. She's fantastic! She's unbeliev-
ably attractive. She is the most beautiful woman I have ever
seen.

DESMOND. Yes, she is lovely isn't she?

RAYMOND. She is so lovely I can barely bear to look upon
her.

DESMOND. Right. So anyway shall we get on with the World
Tour now?

RAYMOND. But look Your Highness! Look at the crowds!
They're all going mad! They all want to talk to her and not
to you basically. You've been totally superseded!!

DESMOND. It's probably just a novelty thing. Um . . .

RAYMOND. No. I think not. In fact, I think she is a modern
icon of our times. That men and women fall in love with her
in a kind of primal primogenital –

DESMOND. Alright, don't go on about it.

RAYMOND. And beside her, you look incredibly fuddy duddy
and boring –

DESMOND. Yes alright –

RAYMOND. – and middle-aged.

DESMOND. Yes, I think we get the point Raymond, thank you.

RAYMOND. I'm only doin' what you wrote Desmond.

DESMOND. Yes, well it was very good! Well done, Raymond. So let's get on shall we?

RAYMOND. Look here she comes now!

RAYMOND *exits.*

DESMOND. Right. People of Australia and New Zealand. I would just like to say . . . hello . . . hello! Just like to say a couple of –

RAYMOND *comes straight back on as* DIANA. *She is in a state of nervous excitement.*

RAYMOND. Hello Charles!! Look how I've transformed from nursery governess to high flyin' sophisticate. This is the life for me Charles! Give me champagne! And Cocktails. And Vol-au-vents.

RAYMOND *stands in front of* DESMOND.

DESMOND. Fabulous. Um . . . may I –

RAYMOND. And Steak Diane!

DESMOND. Yeah!

DESMOND *moves.* RAYMOND *stands in front of him again.*

RAYMOND. So now let's go on to our next country on our World Tour of the World Dominions. To the magical Orient. And in particular – Indonesia!!

Music: Overture to 'The King and I'.

Home of the famous Javanese Temple Dance of the Dance of the Dance of the Seven –

DESMOND. No! We don't have time for that now. Sorry! Cut it! Cut the music!

Music: 'The King and I' stops.

RAYMOND. What?

DESMOND. I've had to cut the Java sequence unfortunately Raymond.

RAYMOND (*stricken*). Cut it!!?

DESMOND. Yes.

RAYMOND. What? No temple dance at all!!?

DESMOND. No!

RAYMOND. But Desmond you promised!!

DESMOND. No!!

RAYMOND. Why?

DESMOND. Are you aware of the time, Raymond! This happens to be one of the most uncomfortable theatres in the entire country. These people have been crammed in here for over an hour!

RAYMOND. But Desmond it was my favourite bit!

DESMOND. So back to Terra Firma. Back to the –

RAYMOND. So where are we now then Desmond?

DESMOND. I'm just about to say Raymond. Back to the United Kingdom.

RAYMOND. Boring!

DESMOND. And Buckingham Palace in the heart of London's Theatreland. Charles is in his office.

RAYMOND *sighs*.

DESMOND. Diana in her boudoir.

RAYMOND. Fascinating!

DESMOND (*whispering urgently into his phone*). Hello. Might I speak with Camilla Parker Knoll please? Thank you.

Meanwhile RAYMOND *as* DIANA *is pacing up and down in her boudoir.*

RAYMOND. I am bored, bored, bored! Ever since we came back from Ostend and New Zealand I want to get out there again! Go on Walkabouts! Having cocktails with the wallabies.

DESMOND. Hello. Yes, it's . . . Prince Charles here. I am calling from Buckingham Palace.

RAYMOND. Bored, bored, bored!

DESMOND. No, I'm not just ringing to say Happy Christmas, Camilla. I want to say –

RAYMOND. I think I'll ring someone up on the Palace telephone. I think I'll ring up Pavarotti or Wayne Sleep.

RAYMOND *grabs the phone receiver from offstage and puts it to his ear.*

DESMOND. I am madly in love with you and always have been!!

RAYMOND *gasps.*

RAYMOND. Oh no! He's on the palace telephone! And he's just said 'I'm madly in love with you'! Who can it be? Shall I listen in? Oh no! I cannot bear to know the truth! What shall I do? Shall I listen in and possibly learn something not to my advantage? Or bury it all under the cupboard? What shall I do!?

RAYMOND *is surprised to find that the* AUDIENCE *starts to offer encouragement and suggestions.*

Hands up who thinks I should listen in? Hands up who thinks I should bury it under the cupboard? Who's not sure?

DESMOND *slams the phone down and marches over to* RAYMOND.

DESMOND. Raymond!! What the hell are you doing?

RAYMOND. Sorry, Desmond!

DESMOND. This is not Whose Line is it Anyway!

RAYMOND. Sorry.

DESMOND. This is not a participatory sequence.

RAYMOND. I wasn't expecting them to all start hagglin'.

DESMOND. Heckling. (*To* AUDIENCE.) And would you not encourage him please! Look at him!

RAYMOND *stands inert.*

He's hopelessly over-excited now! Carry on please Raymond!

RAYMOND. Right! I am going to listen in!

RAYMOND *puts the receiver to his ear again.* DESMOND *picks up the gold phone again.*

DESMOND. Do I have to spell it out? I love you!

RAYMOND *gasps.*

RAYMOND. Oh no! But who can it be?

DESMOND. Yes, Camilla!

RAYMOND. Camilla? Camilla who?

DESMOND. Yes, with you, Camilla Parker Knoll –

RAYMOND (*gasps*). Camilla Parker Knoll!

RAYMOND *stands there stricken as he listens in.*

DESMOND. There is only you. And I can no more live without you than live with you without myself. But I am the Prince of the Wales, Duchess of Cornwall and Mull of Kintyre. Upholder of English family values and the British Library. Besides which, I have two small sons to set an example to. Sorry? Yes we had another. Yes. Anyway, as I was – Two now, yes. But – Two princes yes – But as I was – No I cannot put them in the Tower!!! It's alright. You're overwrought. I'm overwraught.

RAYMOND (*to* AUDIENCE). I'm overwrought.

DESMOND. Yes I am as well.

RAYMOND (*to* AUDIENCE). So am I!

DESMOND. All we can do is engage in sexual relationships of a clandestine and adulterous nature.

RAYMOND (*to* AUDIENCE). Oh no! sexual relationships of a clandestine and industrial nature!!

DESMOND. If that's okay with you. And for this purpose we shall have to find what are known as 'Safe Houses' in order for us to conduct our clandestine and adulterous –

RAYMOND *walks in, straight into* CHARLES*'s office without knocking. He still holds the phone receiver.*

RAYMOND. Hello Charles!

DESMOND. And would you deliver them as soon as possible please. Thank you. (*Puts phone down.*) Just ordering up some new . . . organic vegetables . . . for the new . . . organic vegetable garden. What's the matter? You're looking a bit . . . are you alright?

RAYMOND. Yes thank you.

DESMOND. Anyway, as you know it's Christmas Day –

RAYMOND. Happy Christmas.

DESMOND. And time to listen to my mother's Christmas broadcast to the nation.

RAYMOND. I have decided that this year I – in fact – won't be listening to the Christmas broadcast. Instead I'm going to run amok in the Palace complex.

DESMOND. I beg your pardon?

RAYMOND. Don't try and stop me Charles!

Music: Psycho.

RAYMOND *rushes out of the gold doors.*

DESMOND *picks up the phone.*

DESMOND. Private Secretary. Quick find Princess Diana! She's running amok in the Palace complex! Quick! Find her! Find her!!

DESMOND *charges off through the curtains.*

RAYMOND *charges across the stage, still holding the phone receiver.*

RAYMOND. Don't stop me! Don't stop me! I'm running amok in the Palace complex!

RAYMOND *rushes out.*

Music: last bars of 'God Save the Queen'.

DESMOND *runs in, regains his dignity, collects the handbag and sits behind the table.*

DESMOND. Hello my peoples. I am the Queen Elizabeth and here is my Christmas message to all my people. And I just want to say, let's face it we're all one big family. Which makes me think of my family on Christmas Day. Which is probably exactly like your family I should imagine. With liveried footmen bringing in millions of gifts from our loyal subjects. Later in the day we'd have a huge banquet. Followed by exciting sessions of Racing Demon, Snap –

RAYMOND *appears through the door looking deranged.*

RAYMOND. Excuse me?

DESMOND. – or Happy Families.

RAYMOND *sits at the other end of the table, looks directly into the 'camera'.*

RAYMOND. I'm running amok in the Palace Complex.

DESMOND. Ah! And here is my daughter-in-law the Princess of Wales. (*Picks up a discreet phone.*) Charles, would you pop in here a moment please. Then of course it was bath night with lots of splashing and laughing.

RAYMOND. Everyone thinks being the Princess of Wales is a piece of cake. But it's not. It's far from it actually!

DESMOND (*phone again*). And a couple of Securicor men. Yes, it was very much 'the Simple Life' as the King used to say.

RAYMOND. I'm in a labyrinth I can't get out of! I can't see the wood for the trees!

DESMOND (*phone*). Get a shift on Charles!

RAYMOND. Is anyone aware of what I'm going through?

DESMOND. And finally let us not forget all the families in the world and all their families. Thank you.

RAYMOND. Thank you.

DESMOND. And a very Happy Christmas.

RAYMOND. Happy Christmas.

Music: 'The Man Who Knew Too Much'.

DESMOND *walks to the front.*

DESMOND. And so Prince Charles bore in his breast his terrible secret passion. Known to the Princess of Wales, as we know, though unbeknownst to him that she knew for she knew what he knew but he knew not what she knew. For she knew but would not say and he knew but would not say also.

RAYMOND *storms through the curtains.*

RAYMOND. I'm going out!

DESMOND. Going out! But we've only just moved in! To our new marital home in Kensington Palace Gardens.

RAYMOND. You didn't tell me the others all lived here as well.

DESMOND. Who?

RAYMOND. All the other members of the Royal Family. Princess Margaret. The Duchess of Kent. Princess Alexandra Palace.

DESMOND. Well, she's friendly!

RAYMOND. Yeah, well Ally's Pally, but the rest are drivin' me mad!

DESMOND. They've got to live somewhere.

RAYMOND. Always droppin' round for cups of sugar and cat food. It's driving me barmy! They're all so boring!

DESMOND. Oh are they?

RAYMOND. Yes, they are! And I know exactly why you want to keep me here in the Crystal Palace!

DESMOND. Oh do you!?

RAYMOND. YES!!

DESMOND. Why then?

RAYMOND. Pardon?

DESMOND. Why then?

RAYMOND. Why?

DESMOND. Yes.

> DIANA *nearly tells* CHARLES *she knows about Camilla.*
> *Then decides not.*

RAYMOND. I am . . . not prepared to divulge the wheres and whyfores at this juncture. But I have decided to move out of the marital bedrooms in Kensington Place and not have the breakfast.

DESMOND (*shocked*). Not have the breakfast?

RAYMOND. No!!

DESMOND. But you are the Princess of Wales. You must have the breakfast!

RAYMOND. Get real Charles! I am an Independent Woman! I can do what I wish! In fact I'm not eating anything at the moment. And now I'm going out !

DESMOND. You stay right here, Diana!

RAYMOND. No!

DESMOND. I command you in the name of the House of Fraser!

RAYMOND (*flustered*). Hah! Not even Barbara . . . Fraser could keep me here.

DESMOND. In the name of the House of Windsor!

RAYMOND. Hah! Not even Barbara . . . Windsor could keep me here. Anyway I happen to be going out dancing at a

well-known night club and no-one's going to stop me!
I happen to be going with His Royal Duchess the Princess
of York, who is introducing me to a whole new young
crowd as it happens. So don't bother waitin' up!!!

DESMOND. I WON'T!!

RAYMOND. Good!!

RAYMOND *storms out of the gold doors.*

DESMOND. Meanwhile, next door are the Royal Princes.

DESMOND *and* RAYMOND *become the royal* PRINCES.
RAYMOND *takes the model train and plays with it on the
table.*

RAYMOND. Are they still having a terrible row?

DESMOND (*listens*). No. They've just finished. She's gone
out. He's listening to Classic FM.

RAYMOND. What's going to happen William?

DESMOND. I think we might have to brace ourselves, Harry.

RAYMOND. For what William?

DESMOND. For a separation.

RAYMOND. What's a separation precisely?

DESMOND. You know when you break the coupling and take
the engine off its tender?

RAYMOND. Yes?

DESMOND. Well it's like that.

RAYMOND. What about all the little carriages?

DESMOND. They stay together. Alright?

RAYMOND. Yes. (*He looks at his engine.*) Will you look at
my Flying Scotsman now William?

DESMOND. Of course I will, Harry.

RAYMOND. Thank you.

DESMOND. Meanwhile, in Charles's office –

DESMOND sits at the table. He is CHARLES *again. He picks up the gold phone.*

DESMOND. Hello is that the Duke of Edinburgh? Oh hello. This is your son here. Charles. Yes. Um, I know we've never actually spoken before but I was wondering if I could possibly ask you for some . . . sounds silly after all these years but . . . some advice on a personal . . . Absolutely. Fair enough. It's very late in the evening. I fully understand. I'm sorry. My fault. Goodbye.

Replaces the phone.

Music: Blues from Taxi Driver Score by Bernard Herrmann.

RAYMOND *wanders sultrily in and sits at the table. Seconds later* DESMOND *joins him and sits sultrily too.*

RAYMOND. Well, this is more like it, I must say. Champagne! Dancing! Nightclubs! Dressing up as lady police women!

DESMOND. This is the life isn't it, Diana!

RAYMOND. It certainly is, Yorkie.

DESMOND. So . . . what do you like best about this new kind of lifestyle we're leading? If you had to make a choice?

RAYMOND. Um . . .

DESMOND. Between the wild dancing and the massive spending.

RAYMOND (*thinks*). The wild dancing. What would yours be in your opinion?

DESMOND. In my opinion?

RAYMOND. Yes!

DESMOND. The massive spending. But then I am on the edge of a nervous breakdown.

RAYMOND. I thought I was!

An uneasy moment of competition.

DESMOND. No I am now as well.

RAYMOND. Oh! But –

DESMOND. Anyway shall we do some wild dancing now then?

RAYMOND. Alright Corgi! let's do some wild dancing!

Wild disco music.

They start doing some wild dancing.

DESMOND. But what we need now is some attractive young men to do wild dancing with.

RAYMOND. Yeah!!

DESMOND. Look here comes some young attractive young dancin' men.

RAYMOND. Yes they certainly are Porkie.

DESMOND. Yorkie.

RAYMOND. Korkie.

DESMOND. Yorkie!

RAYMOND. Yorkie!

DESMOND. So let's go and do some wild dancing with them then!

RAYMOND. But stop!

Wild disco music stops abruptly.

RAYMOND *is suddenly transfixed.*

Who is that who's just walked into the nightclub?

DESMOND. That is Captain James Hewitt the well-known ginger-haired lifeguard. Shall I ask him over?

RAYMOND. Alright.

DESMOND. Wait here.

RAYMOND. Righto.

DESMOND *walks to the back, takes the lifeguard's hat from its plinth, puts it on and returns immediately as* CAPTAIN JAMES HEWITT.

DESMOND. Hello.

RAYMOND. Hello. I understand you are a well-known ginger-haired lifeguard.

DESMOND. That would be correct Your Highness.

RAYMOND. You save people on the beach?

DESMOND. No, that's a . . . er . . . a coast guard. (RAYMOND *looks blank.*) I am a life-guard.

RAYMOND. Yeah. Anyway, would you be kind enough to report to my Imperial Palace at Kensington High Street at two tomorrow afternoon please?

DESMOND. Certainly Your Highness.

RAYMOND. Thank you. And –

DESMOND. Yes?

RAYMOND (*seductively*). Don't be late.

MUSIC: 'The Man Who Knew Too Much' – Prelude.

The table is now PRINCESS DIANA*'s office.* RAYMOND *sits behind the desk.* DESMOND *knocks on the table.*

RAYMOND. Come in.

DESMOND *mimes opening and closing the door.*

DESMOND. You asked to see me Your Highness?

RAYMOND. That's right I did actually. What was your name again?

DESMOND. Captain James Hewitt Your Highness.

RAYMOND (*feigning indifference*). Ah yes that's right. Now look here Captain Suet – do take your hat off by the way.

DESMOND *takes the hat off and puts it on the table.*

DESMOND. Thank you.

RAYMOND. I should just like to say you are the most attractive man I have ever met.

DESMOND. Thank you very much.

RAYMOND. In other words, what I'm driving at here James is I'm very keen to engage in a powerful no-holds barred sexual union with you personally.

DESMOND. Right.

RAYMOND. I hope you are not shocked by the explicit nature of my dialogue.

DESMOND. Um . . .

RAYMOND. But I am undergoing various trainings to enable me to express myself as a sexually assertive woman. (*Asserts herself.*) I am a sexually assertive woman!

DESMOND. Thank you.

RAYMOND *begins to move seductively round the table.* DESMOND *starts to look nervous.*

RAYMOND. Do you want me James? Tell me! Tell me! I am yearnin' and yearnin'!! James! James! James Hewitt!

DESMOND (*suddenly addresses the* AUDIENCE). And so it was –

RAYMOND. Oh James, I say!!

DESMOND. Steady, Raymond!

RAYMOND *attempts to embrace* DESMOND.

RAYMOND. James Hewitt!

DESMOND. Raymond!

DESMOND *panics and recoils. He straightens his clothing.*

For God's sake!!

RAYMOND. Sorry.

DESMOND. And so it was the romance –

RAYMOND. So we're not doing the bed scene then Desmond?

DESMOND. No obviously not no. And so it was –

RAYMOND. I was dreading the bed scene Desmond!

DESMOND. Yes . And so –

RAYMOND. Phew!

DESMOND. Right . . . and so it was the romance of Diana the Princess Royal of Wales and Captain Sir James Hewitt blossomed into romance.

Romantic music: Mozart Flute and Harp Concerto.

RAYMOND. Dear James! I can hardly believe we have known each other only three weeks!

DESMOND. Yes.

RAYMOND. You've made me happy as a handbag.

DESMOND. Sandboy.

RAYMOND. Sandbag.

DESMOND. Sandboy.

RAYMOND. Handboy. Oh tell me our love will have no end James!

DESMOND. Our love will have no end Your Highness.

RAYMOND. Tell me again.

DESMOND. Our love will have no –

RAYMOND *knock knock knocks on the table.*

RAYMOND. Who's that?

DESMOND (*turns his back*). It's me Prince Charles.

Music: 'Psycho' prelude.

TOGETHER. Oh no! Prince Charles!!!

RAYMOND. Coming!! Quick James! Hide in the ensuite toilet and bathroom facilities.

RAYMOND *pushes* DESMOND *through the curtain.*
DESMOND *runs round behind the central doors.*
RAYMOND *opens the doors.* DESMOND *walks in as* CHARLES.

RAYMOND. Hello Charles.

DESMOND. Hello Diana! You was a long time opening the door. Do you have something to hide?

RAYMOND. No!

DESMOND (*picking up lifeguard's hat*). So what is that then in this case? What is this then in that case?

RAYMOND. Um . . .

DESMOND. It's a lifeguard's hat, isn't it?

RAYMOND. No.

DESMOND. Don't try and pull the wool over my eyes, Diana! It's a lifeguard's hat and you know it. And if I'm not very much mistaken it will have the owner's name in it.

RAYMOND. How do you know?

DESMOND. Because they all have to have their names in them because the hats are all so similar. Ah! 'J. Hewitt (Captain)'. So where is he then this Captain Hewitt! (*Suddenly realises and points.*) There's someone in your ensuite bathrooom and toilet facilities! Come out of there Captain Hewitt!

RAYMOND. It's not what you think Charles. It's not Captain Hewitt!

DESMOND. So who is it then?

RAYMOND. It's –

DESMOND. Yes?

RAYMOND. The cleaning lady!

DESMOND. Oh really? Well, I was hopin' it might be possible to discuss the possibilities of a reconciliation.

RAYMOND (*wrong footed*). Oh! Was you?

DESMOND. Yes! But clearly you're otherwise 'engaged!'

RAYMOND. But it's all perfectly innocent!

DESMOND. Innocent my foot!

RAYMOND. It is!!

DESMOND. And all these other leading men you been seeing such as Captain Will Carling Blacklabel. Was they all innocent as well?

RAYMOND. Alright then – BAT EARS!!

DESMOND *gasps.*

RAYMOND. What about . . . Camilla!!!

DESMOND (*gasps even more*). I don't know who you're talking about!!

RAYMOND. In that case in my personal opinion we have no other option than to get . . .

DESMOND. What?

RAYMOND. What?

DESMOND. What?

RAYMOND. What?

DESMOND. What?

RAYMOND. DIVORCED!!

DESMOND (*gasps*). Alright then!! DIVORCE IT IS!!

RAYMOND (*gasps*). I didn't mean it!

DESMOND. No! I'm afraid it's too late for that now, Diana! Divorce is what you said and Divorce is what you're gettin'.

RAYMOND. I was upset!

DESMOND (*looking steely*). Tough bananas Diana! It's too late! It's just too late!

Music: 'Panorama' Theme.

DESMOND *and* RAYMOND *move the chairs to the front of the stage and sit down facing one another.*

DESMOND. Hello. This is the BBC and welcome to Panorama. And tonight we have something just a little bit different. An exclusive interview with Her Royal Highness the Princess of Wales. Your Royal Highness.

RAYMOND. Hello.

DESMOND. Hello. So anyway let's get crackin'. Here comes the questions. Ready?

RAYMOND. Yep.

DESMOND. One. Do you feel totally unappreciated by the Royal Family?

RAYMOND. Yes I do. They have made my life unmitigated hell.

DESMOND. Thank you. Next question. Would you like to be the Queen of England.

RAYMOND. No. Not the Queen of England but the Queen of Hearts.

DESMOND. Thank you. And the final question and the only one we're really interested in – Did you in fact have an affair with Captain James Hewitt of an intimate nature allegedly? And I've started so you can finish.

RAYMOND. Yes I did.

DESMOND. Thank you.

RAYMOND. In fact I adored him. (*She looks directly at camera.*)

DESMOND. So anyway –

RAYMOND. And I hope you heard that Charles!

An awkward moment.

DESMOND. Right. So anyway that brings us to the end of this special live edition of Panorama. So it's goodnight from me and goodnight from her.

RAYMOND. Goodnight.

Music: 'A battuta' from Chain by Lutoslawski.

RAYMOND *shoves the table to the side and plonks the throne in the centre. He grabs the handbag.*

RAYMOND. Couldn't you have stopped her, Charles?

DESMOND. No Mother, I couldn't stop her!

RAYMOND. No you never could, could you!! Saying all that
about the Royal Family! Saying we drove her barmy!
Ridiculous! How could we drive anyone barmy! I'll tell you
one thing, when we get the Labour in we're going to have
words about the BBC. How could we drive anyone barmy!

DESMOND. Ridiculous!

RAYMOND. And now she's asking for what?

DESMOND. Forty-six million.

RAYMOND. Forty-six million pounds! Does she think we're
made of money?

DESMOND. We are made of money.

RAYMOND. She can have fifteen.

DESMOND. Fifteen pounds? That's not very gener –

RAYMOND. Fifteen million! And how are we going to raise
that might I ask Charles.

DESMOND. Sell something?

RAYMOND. What?

DESMOND. Cornwall?

RAYMOND. Sell Cornwall!? We can't sell Cornwall!!

DESMOND. We could sell it to France.

RAYMOND. Don't be ridiculous!

DESMOND. It's quite French now. There's the Cornish
Riviera, for example. St. Ives. Or – Saint Ives –

RAYMOND. Will you shut up about Cornwall! I tell you! This
year! (*Shakes head.*) We've had the England Revenue on
our backs! We've had Yorkie topless! We've had – Phew it's
hot. Open the door would you Charles?

DESMOND. Certainly.

RAYMOND. We've had Edward leaving the Marines!

CHARLES *opens the gold doors. Smoke pours out. We see red flickering flames and hear a dreadful roaring noise. He slams the doors and reels round in a shocked state. The* QUEEN *has noticed nothing and carries on regardless.*

RAYMOND. We bought him that lovely Marine outfit! Did he ever wear it?

CHARLES – *not believing what he saw – opens the doors again. More smoke and flames. He slams the doors again.*

DESMOND. Um . . .

RAYMOND. I say did he ever wear it? Once!

DESMOND. Er . . .

RAYMOND. God it's hot! Will you open the door!!

DESMOND. Um . . .

RAYMOND. Alright I'll open the door!

The QUEEN *opens the doors. The flames and the dreadful roaring have taken hold now. Smoke pours through the doors. They are both forced back into the room.*

RAYMOND. Bloody Norah! The whole of Windsor Castle's going up.

CHARLES *manages to slam the doors shut. The* QUEEN *is very angry now.*

RAYMOND. This is your fault, Charles! This is a terrible terrible year we're havin'!

DESMOND. Yes, it is all my fault. I'm very very sorry.

RAYMOND. In fact, it is my personal opinon that this year has truly been my Anus!

DESMOND. Raymond!!!

RAYMOND. What?

DESMOND. Annus!

RAYMOND. Pardon?

DESMOND. Annus!!

RAYMOND. Anus.

DESMOND. Annus !!! Annus horrib –

RAYMOND. . . . Horribib . . . Hobbi . . . Hob . . .

DESMOND. Horribilis!

RAYMOND. Hobbiribilibibilis . . .

DESMOND. HORRIBILIS!!

RAYMOND. It's very hard to say actually, Desmond! Horribibiribili –

DESMOND. Just say it Raymond!

RAYMOND. horribibibillibibilsibil –

DESMOND. SAY IT!

RAYMOND. NO !!!

DESMOND. What?

RAYMOND. NO I WON'T !!!

DESMOND. I beg your pardon?

RAYMOND. You been gettin' at me ever since we started you been gettin' at me! Well I've had it with you Desmond! They've had it with you! Everyone's had it with you! You say you've had close contact with the Royal Family. Oh really?

DESMOND. Raymond –

RAYMOND. Well, if I was the Royal Family I'd give you a very wide berth!

DESMOND. Oh would you?

RAYMOND. Yes! If you want to know.

DESMOND. Well there's a number of things I should like to say to you Raymond if you want to know. One –

RAYMOND. Particularly after that terrible poem you wrote!

DESMOND. Pardon?

RAYMOND. That terrible poem!

DESMOND. What poem?

RAYMOND. The one you wrote to the Queen.

DESMOND (*turns to the* AUDIENCE). And anyway on now –

RAYMOND. When you was proposing yourself as Poet
Laureate.

DESMOND (*laughs loudly*). Raymond! That is completely
fallacious nonsense!

RAYMOND. You did though.

DESMOND. I don't know what you're talking about.

RAYMOND. And you was replied to by that horrible lady.

DESMOND. What horrible lady?

RAYMOND. That horrible lady in waiting –

DESMOND. Honourable Lady in Waiting Raymond! She
wrote me a very nice letter as it happens.

RAYMOND. It wasn't from the Queen though was it
Desmond?

DESMOND. It was dictated by the Queen!

RAYMOND. Dear Mr Dingle, your poem was the worst
bloody thing I've ever read in my life. Best wishes the
Queen.

DESMOND. Shut your face Raymond!

Suddenly RAYMOND *whips the poem out of his pocket.
He runs to the front of the stage.*

RAYMOND (*reads*).
O Queen how thou dost deserve that name –

DESMOND. Where d'you get that?

RAYMOND (*reads*).
Cos you are on high and full of fame –

DESMOND *tries to grab the poem.*

DESMOND. Raym –

RAYMOND (*reads on*).
Look at all the good deeds you done
O thou art great and so's your Mum.

DESMOND. Give it back Raymond!

RAYMOND.
Your smile is like a lovely flower
And though some people think you're dour
I don't think so. Oh dear no –

DESMOND *grabs the poem and tears it up.*

DESMOND. Alright that's it!!! You seem to be entertaining the crowds very well on your own Raymond – so I'll just leave you to it.

RAYMOND. What?

DESMOND. I don't wish to cramp your style Raymond. So I'll just bow out now!

RAYMOND. Bow out?

DESMOND. You obviously feel you're capable of doing the rest of the show on your own so I look forward to seeing it.

DESMOND *walks into the audience.*

RAYMOND. Rest of the show?

DESMOND. Go on then Raymond!

RAYMOND. Where are you goin' then?

DESMOND. I'll sit here.

RAYMOND. In the audience?

DESMOND. Yes. With Joe Public, Raymond.

DESMOND *squeezes into a row.*

DESMOND. Shove up would you please. Get on with it Raymond! Hurry up! You're losing 'em!

RAYMOND. Good evening ladies and gentlemen. Good evening Desmond. You will by now have noticed that I am

clothed in something rather unus . . . (*Starts trotting.*) Hello
Prince Charles! Are you Prince Charles? I am as it happens.
You're very attractive (*Stops trotting.*) . . . Oh James! James
Hewitt! James Hewitt! (*He kicks the chair. Then suddenly
gets a brilliant idea.*) And now! Ladies and Gentlemen the
most fascinating moment in the whole of the evening.
The famous Javanese Temple Dance of the Dance of the
Dance of the Seven Veils. After three please. One, two,
three, four –

Music: Iranian dance music.

At last RAYMOND *dances the Dance of the Seven Veils.
At the end of which he receives a standing ovation. He is
overwhelmed and starts bowing excitedly.*

DESMOND *can contain himself no longer. He leaps up and
rushes back on stage.* RAYMOND *is still bowing to the*
AUDIENCE *who are clamouring for more.*

DESMOND. Alright! Stop this! Stop it! Stop it! Raymond!!
You have reduced the entire performance to an End of the
Pier concert party. To a song and dance routine!!!

RAYMOND. Sorry Desmond. I got a bit over-excited actually.

DESMOND. Yes you did!

RAYMOND. So what shall we do now then?

DESMOND. We'd better do the final scene, Raymond.

RAYMOND. Right. So what scene's that then please Desmond
please?

DESMOND. The Saville Road scene.

RAYMOND. Saville Road?

DESMOND. Saville Row!

RAYMOND. Saville Row. Yes. Right. Thank you.

*They both exit through the left and right curtains. Then
appear simultaneously from either side. They stop, suddenly
surprised and embarrassed. It's been a while.*

DESMOND. Oh!

RAYMOND. Oh!

DESMOND. Hello Diana.

RAYMOND. Hello Charles.

DESMOND. I'm just coming out of my exclusive tailors where I buy all my suits as you know.

RAYMOND. Yes.

DESMOND. So what are you doing?

RAYMOND. I am going to see an holistic health practitioner who is benevolent and kindly and full of wisdom which is all one needs really.

DESMOND. That's good.

RAYMOND. So where are you going then?

DESMOND. To my . . . solicitors. To talk about the . . . er . . . marriage possibilities to . . . erm . . .

RAYMOND. Oh. Right.

DESMOND. Anyway . . . (*They look at one another.*) I'm very very sorry.

RAYMOND. What for?

DESMOND. For not loving you as I should of. I'm afraid I was a bit of a . . . bit of a –

RAYMOND. Charlie?

DESMOND. Bit of a Charlie yes. Sorry.

RAYMOND. I'm sorry I called you Bat Ears.

DESMOND. They was probably the least of your problems –

RAYMOND. What was?

DESMOND. My ears. Anyway . . .

RAYMOND. Anyway I am now able to say this to you owing as a result of the various therapies and whatnot I been doing. I will never love anyone as I loved you and I never will.

DESMOND. Can't think why.

RAYMOND. No nor can I. I saw you on the telly the other night. Whittling on about the state of British architecture.

DESMOND. Oh right.

RAYMOND. You looked so sad and lost and lonely. (*Pause.*) We never had much in common.

DESMOND. No.

RAYMOND. Except our two lovely boys.

DESMOND. Except our two lovely boys.

RAYMOND. Perhaps that is why we was brought together.

DESMOND. Yes.

RAYMOND. Everything's meant in my opinion.

DESMOND. Hope so.

They ponder this.

RAYMOND. I'll probably never see you again.

DESMOND. You going away?

RAYMOND. I am yes.

DESMOND. Right.

RAYMOND. Ooh! Looks like rain.

DESMOND. Huh! Always the way. Just when things start looking up –

TOGETHER. Down comes the rain! Ah well!

Pause as neither knows what to say.

RAYMOND. Bye then.

DESMOND. Goodbye.

They start to separate. Moving back towards the curtain entrances.

RAYMOND. Don't do anything I wouldn't do!

DESMOND. Not if I can help it!

RAYMOND. Okay. Bye.

DESMOND. Bye.

RAYMOND. Bye.

DESMOND. Bye.

They disappear through the red velvet curtains.

Music: The Warsaw Concerto.

The End.